Newbridge Disco

A Rain Forest Adventure

Christine and Anton Economos

A Rain Forest Adventure
ISBN: 1-58273-720-7

Program Author: Dr. Brenda Parkes, Literacy Expert
Content Reviewer: Dr. Robert Anderson, Research Scientist,
Canadian Museum of Nature, Ottawa, Ontario
Teacher Reviewer: Carmen Alvarez-Rodriguez, Austin ISD, Austin TX

Written by Christine and Anton Economos
Editorial and Design Assistance by Curriculum Concepts

Many thanks to our rain forest guides Jesse Dingot, Juan Torres,
Abelardo Chacón, and Leo Godinez.

Newbridge Educational Publishing
11 East 26th Street, New York, NY 10010
www.newbridgeonline.com

Printed in Canada.

Cover Photograph: Jaguarundi
Table of Contents Photograph: Anton up in the canopy

Photo Credits
Cover: Tom Brakefield/DRK Photo; Contents page: Christine Economos; Pages 4-5: (background) J. C. Carton/Bruce Coleman, Inc., (inset) Stephen Ogilvy; Page 6: Christine Economos; Page 7: Christine Economos; Page 8: (inset) Christine Economos; Pages 8-9: Drew Thate/Bruce Coleman, Inc.; Page 10: Gerry Ellis/Minden Pictures; Page 11: Michael Fogden/Bruce Coleman, Inc.; Page 12: C. C. Lockwood/DRK Photo; Page 13: E. R. Degginger/Bruce Coleman, Inc.; Pages 14-15: IFA-Bilderteam/Bruce Coleman, Inc.; Pages 16-17: Gregory G. Dimijan/Photo Researchers, Inc.; Page 18: Christine Economos; Pages 18-19: Christine Economos; Page 19: Christine Economos; Page 20: Stephen J. Krasemann/DRK Photo; Page 21: (top) Mark Moffett/Minden Pictures, (bottom) Michael Fogden/DRK Photo; Page 22: (left) Michael Fogden/DRK Photo, (right) Michael Fogden/DRK Photo; Page 23: Gregory G. Dimijan/Photo Researchers, Inc.; Page 24: Michael Fogden/DRK Photos; Pages 24-25: Gregory Dimijan/Photo Researchers, Inc.; Page 26: Christine Economos; Page 27: (left) Joe McDonald/Bruce Coleman, Inc., (right) Stephen J. Krasemann/DRK Photo; Page 28: Stephen J. Krasemann/DRK Photo; Pages 28-29: Alan D. Carey/Photo Researchers, Inc.; Page 30: (top left) Michael Fogden/Bruce Coleman, Inc., (top right) Michael Fogden/DRK Photo, (bottom) Frans Lanting/Minden Pictures; Page 31: (left) Christine Economos, (right) Tim Davis/Photo Researchers, Inc.

Maps/Illustrations: Steve Stankiewicz, Page 31;
Tracy Zungola, Pages 5, 6, 11, 15, 21

10 9 8 7 6 5 4

Table of Contents

We're in Costa Rica

The plane bumps along the runway and rolls to a stop. My son, Anton, and I look out the plane window.

We see green, grassy rolling hills, with tall mountains rising in the background. We have just landed in Costa Rica.

"Got everything?" I ask.

"Yes," says Anton. He finishes drawing a map in his journal and slips it into his backpack. "I'm filling the rest of the journal with our experiences," he says.

This is the beginning of our great rain forest adventure. We can't wait.

Costa Rica is about 2,000 miles from New York City, where Chris and Anton (shown above) live. Costa Rica has a warm tropical climate.

New York City
our home
USA
Atlantic
Ocean
MEXICO
Miami
We stopped
here.
Pacific
Ocean
COSTA
RICA!

We spend the night in San José, the capital, which is a very busy city. In the morning, we pack our backpacks. We also pay close attention to what we wear so we will be comfortable in the heat. Then we drive to La Fortuna, a village in the North. Jesse, our guide, is waiting for us.

"Ready to visit the rain forest?" he asks. "Horseback is the only way to get there."

"I've never been on a horse before," says Anton.

Jesse smiles and says, "Your horse is named *Perezoso*. It means 'lazy' in Spanish. I don't think he'll give you any trouble."

We ride by areas where the forest has been cut down for cattle grazing. We pass groves of trees and go through several small streams. While we ride, Jesse tells us that we are going to be in a humid tropical rain forest called the Orlich Reserve. Each year, it gets about nine feet of rain! Miami, Florida, a U.S. city that has a lot of rain, gets only about half that amount.

Riding through mud and streams, it will take about 45 minutes to get to Orlich Reserve.

In the Rain Forest

It is quiet and still. We are surrounded by green. Only a small amount of light filters through the trees to the forest floor. Jesse tells us there are at least a dozen forest zones in Costa Rica.

"The zones have different climates, altitudes, and plants and animals," he says. "Later on, we will visit a forest near the coast that is drier and gets less rain."

"I thought all rain forests were alike," says Anton.

"There are rain forests throughout the world," says Jesse. "Each has its own unique plants and animals."

Many of the plants and animals in the rain forest are hard to see, but a guide can help point them out.

The massive roots of this tree are called buttress roots. They spread out to get nutrients from the top layer of soil and also help support the tree.

Many people think that the rain forest has very rich soil. But only the top four inches or so are full of nutrients. Under that top layer is clay. For that reason, many of the trees have wide spreading roots to steady them. They do not send their roots deep into the ground. Instead, their roots form a web just under the surface of the forest floor. That way they can benefit more from the nutrients in the topsoil.

As we walk along the forest path, Jesse shows us a snake wrapped around a plant. It probably had a meal recently, and is sleeping. It is a golden eyelash viper. He says that it is very poisonous, but as long as we leave it alone, it won't bother us.

Like all snakes, this viper doesn't have eyelids. Its eyes are visible even when it sleeps.

From reading about rain forests, I'd expected to see a lot of animals. But after we saw the snake, we didn't see any animals for about an hour. Jesse tells us it's because we are on the forest floor, where there is little sun and rain. Most of the animals live higher up in the trees, where they get more sun and water.

Jesse points to some plants on the forest floor that have big broad leaves. "This is so they can collect as much sun as possible," he says.

Just then we hear birds calling to one another. We see flashes of blue and orange dart across the path. Toucans!

Toucans use their long colorful beaks to collect and crush fruits and nuts. Their beaks are hollow, so they aren't too heavy.

These yellow-naped Amazon parrots are some of the most intelligent and noisiest birds of the rain forest.

We hear squawking in the trees above. It takes time to focus our binoculars and see what the fuss is about. Two of the toucans are sitting calmly on a tree branch. We see two small green parrots flying frantically around them, squawking loudly.

"What's going on?" asks Anton.

"It looks like the toucans are raiding the parrots' nest," says Jesse.

A few minutes later, we see and hear some monkeys in a tree. Hearing the loud racket they make, we can understand why they are called howler monkeys. We are lucky to see them in the understory. Most of the time, these monkeys stay up in the canopy. Two snarl at us and bare their teeth. We quickly snap a picture and move on.

Howler monkeys are so loud that they can be heard as far as two miles away.

"We'll see more animals in the canopy," says Jesse. "The canopy gets the most sun. Much of the rainwater stays in the canopy. About 70 percent of the plants and animals in a rain forest live in the canopy."

"How can that be?" Anton asks.

"You'll see," says Jesse.

Up in the Canopy

We come to a ladder and begin the long climb to a platform. It is 120 feet above the forest floor. As we climb up, we pass through the understory and are as high up as the howler monkeys were. Here the plants are less dense. Their leaves are smaller, because there is more sunlight here than on the forest floor. Many of these plants are fighting their way to the top, where they can get the most sunlight and water. Finally we reach the platform.

Spider monkeys are amazing acrobats. They swing through the forest using their arms, legs, and tails.

Before they start climbing, Anton and Chris get hooked up to their harnesses.

A strong, 300-foot-long metal cable, called a zip line, connects our tree with another. Six trees are connected this way. Jesse helped to build the platforms and zip lines. They were built in a way that does not harm the trees. The ladders, platforms, and zip lines are attached to the trees with metal cables that have a thick rubber covering. That way no metal touches the tree.

We move from tree to tree over the forest canopy on these zip lines. Our harnesses have big clips that lock over the cable. Then off we go! We sail across the canopy. It feels like we're flying. We wear heavy gloves to protect our hands.

Anton holds on as he moves across the canopy. He is about 120 feet above the ground.

Brightly colored orchids and bromeliads grow together on tree limbs and trunks.

The big story in the canopy is the plants. There are plants everywhere! Mosses, bromeliads, and orchids grow on every branch. Long vines called *lianas* hang from the trees. Heavy rainfall and wind bring all the nutrients these plants need to survive. In turn, these plants provide nutrients and shelter for many animals and insects.

Poison dart frogs come up from the forest floor to place their tadpoles in the pools of water collected inside bromeliads.

As we zip from platform to platform, we see colorful insects everywhere. We see butterflies, dragonflies, caterpillars, and many unusual beetles. Some have horns and stingers. On the platform, we use our binoculars to search for animals in the canopy. Anton spies something brown and green and furry. He hands the binoculars to Jesse.

"Ah," says Jesse. "It's a sloth."

"Why is its back all green?" asks Anton.

"Because the climate is so moist and warm," says Jesse, "algae grows on its fur. The green helps the sloth blend in with its surroundings. Because they move so slowly, we call them *perezosos*."

Insects' bright colors let their enemies know that they are poisonous.

Since sloths are born in the canopy, one of the first things they learn is to hang on.

"Lazy, just like my horse," says Anton.

We get on our horses and go back to La Fortuna. Tomorrow we will visit a very different rain forest, Manuel Antonio National Park, which is on the Pacific Coast.

Rain Forest by the Sea

Butterflies are everywhere at Manuel Antonio National Park! It is hotter and more humid here. Because it is at a lower altitude and has a different climate, we'll see different plants and animals.

Fifty years ago, the hardwood trees in this area were cut down. Since that time, the forest has been recovering. Saplings from trees that were cut down are starting to grow, creating a new generation of hardwood trees. But it is difficult for a rain forest to recover fully. That will take many, many more years.

Morpho butterflies like this one love to spend the day in the sun. At night they hang from trees or the undersides of leaves.

A butterfly lands on Anton's shoulder. He raises his hand and it hops on. It looks just like a dead leaf! He puts it on a tree branch far away from the many lizards darting around on the sandy forest floor. Some lizards are so well camouflaged that you don't notice them right away.

There are crabs on the forest floor, too—millions of them! They are red and black, with beautiful purple claws. We see something running and can't

When butterflies rest, they fold up their wings behind them. Even some of the most colorful butterflies blend in by showing only the dark underside of their wings.

Although basilisk lizards can run across water on their hind legs, they spend more time resting on tree branches.

Colorful land crabs live inside the rain forest. But they must return to the sea to lay their eggs.

believe our eyes! It's a green lizard standing upright and running only on its hind legs. It's a basilisk. I've read that basilisks can run across water this way. I didn't know that they could do this on land. Maybe we're the first ones to witness this!

Agoutis can run quickly but stay very still when they sense danger.

We spot a rodent called an agouti. It looks injured, so we find a park ranger. He says he'll take the animal to the *Jardin Gaia*, an organization dedicated to preserving the rain forest and its animals. There, the agouti will be treated and released back into the forest.

We've seen two rain forests, and even gotten to help a rain forest animal. But now it's time for Anton and me to get ready to fly back home.

The next morning, we're in a cab hurtling along a dusty road that leads to the small airport. Suddenly, something leaps across the road in front of us. It is a large black cat with a long tail. It disappears into the tall grass.

Jaguarundis are so shy and secretive that scientists don't know exactly how many of these endangered cats exist.

"That was a jaguarundi," says the cabdriver. "I have lived here 30 years. I have seen just one other. It is very rare to see one. They stay away from where people are, and usually only walk around at night."

I'm filled with happiness. We've seen the jaguarundi. But I'm even happier to know jaguarundis still exist.

On the plane home, I ask Anton if he would like to come back to Costa Rica.

"Would I!" he answers. "When?"

More Rain Forest Facts

Fungi

These tiny umbrellas are actually mushrooms growing on the forest floor. Mushrooms and other types of fungi help return nutrients to the forest canopy by breaking down dead leaves and other dead plant parts.

White-faced Capuchin Monkey

White-faced Capuchin monkeys are one of the most intelligent kinds of monkeys. They are great climbers and stay in the trees most of the time, coming down to drink water.

Jaguar

Jaguars are the largest cats found in the Americas. Because jaguars have been hunted so much, there are only an estimated 15,000 left in the wild.

Websites

To explore other rain forest topics, log on to these websites:

www.ran.org/kids_action

www.rainforest.org

www.mamamedia.com/activities/my_planet

Plant Diversity

Anton stands happily surrounded by just some of the many plants that make up the rain forest understory.

Scarlet Macaws

Scarlet macaws are among the largest and most beautiful of the rain forest parrots.

Dots on this map show the places that Chris and Anton visited.

Index